Far-Fetched Pets

YOUR
PET
BEAR

By Bobbie Hamsa

Illustrations by Tom Dunnington

Consultant:
  Roger E. Chudzik
  Bear keeper
  Lincoln Park Zoo, Chicago

 CHILDRENS PRESS, CHICAGO

CAUTION
Far-fetched pets should not be kept in your house or apart-
ment or yard. Don't ask for one for your birthday or
Christmas. Go to the zoo or visit the library. There you can
learn more about your favorite far-fetched pet.

Library of Congress Cataloging in Publication Data

Hamsa, Bobbi.
    Your pet bear.

    (Far-fetched pets)
    SUMMARY: Discusses the advantages of having a
bear for a pet, such as his ability to dig a good
hole and eat all the foods that one hates, and gives
instructions for his general care and housing.
    [1. Bears—Anecdotes, facetiae, satire, etc.]
I. Dunnington, Tom. II. Title. III. Series.
PZ7.H1887Yn   [E]   79-24938
ISBN 0-516-03351-4

    4 5 6 7 8 9 10 11 12 R 88 87 86 85 84 83

This is a bear.

An American Black Bear.

He is not always black.

He comes in different shades of yellow and brown.

Pretend that he is your pet.

He has thick, shaggy fur.
Big, sharp teeth.
Bigger, sharper claws.

Huckmorton?

Neru? Shaggy? Fred?

Adolph? King?

Bob?

And almost no tail at all.
What will you name your pet bear?

5

Menu
• Mouse Muffin
• Fly Fricasee
• Pine Cone Pie
• Buggy Pudding
• Grass Goulasch
• Carrot Crunch

6

CARE AND FEEDING OF YOUR PET

Bears eat EVERYTHING.

Fruits, vegetables, bugs, leaves, grass, and mice.

Even pinecones and clam shells if they're really hungry.

For a treat, have mom fix squirrel stuffed with carrots and covered with honey gravy.

But don't let him eat too much. Squirrel is very fattening.

Once every year or so you'll want
to groom your pet.
This is very simple.

Cover him with mud.
Let it dry.

Then let him scratch it off.
This gets rid of old fur.
And new fleas.
It also helps take some of the
stink off.

Your bear will need a quiet place
to sleep.

A cave is best.

Or a basement.

Or perhaps you have a hollow tree?

He could sleep with you, but he's a very messy roommate.

Besides, it might make your teddy jealous.

If your bear is young, he's smaller than you are.

But in two short years, he'll be as tall as your dad.

Think about where you will put your bear.

Your bear can't see or hear very well.

So don't bother taking him to movies.

And say "no" when he asks to drive.

Two things really scare your bear.
Porcupines.
And quicksand.
So before he moves in, hide your mother's pincushion.
And ask dad to drain the swamp.

Play with your bear.
He likes tag.
And tumbling.
But his favorite game is "Hide 'N' Seek" (because he finds you every time).

Take him to the river.
He dearly loves to swim.
No one's better at catching fish—
and he doesn't even need a pole.

20

One final thing . . .
your bear loves to travel.

He has lots of cousins in
Yellowstone Park.

So if you go, take him along for
a visit.

TRAINING

With a little training, your bear
can be very useful.

He can dig a dandy hole . . .

give your friends some wild
"bear-back" rides . . .

sniff out Mom's hiding places for
candy and gum . . .
    hug Aunt Gertrude *for* you.

He'll eat all the foods you hate . . .
scratch itchy places on your back . . .
and make the scariest monster
on Halloween.

Best of all, your bear can make
your brother do W-H-A-T-E-V-E-R you
want him to!

Your bear is a pretty good climber.
So he can put baby birds back up
in trees . . . or bring frightened
kittens down.

He can hang Christmas lights around
the house . . . and reach the tip-top
kitchen cupboard.

If you get lost in the forest, your bear will find food. Nuts. Berries. And other wild things. He may even share with you.

These are only a few of the things your pet can do.

Can you think of more?

If you take good care of him, your bear will live maybe 25 years.

And he'll be the best pet you ever had.

Facts about your pet American Black Bear (*Euarctos americanus*)

Size at birth: 10 to 14 inches long; 12 to 18 ounces

Number of newborn: 1 to 4, two are very common

Average size when grown: males are about 6 feet when standing on their hind
legs, weigh about 400 pounds

Type of food eaten: mostly roots, berries, and leaves. They will eat fish and
sometimes carrion (dead animals).

Expected lifespan: 15 to 25 years

Names—male: boar or he-bear
female: sow, she-bear, or dam
young: cub
group: Bears are most commonly found as solitary animals.
Bears form in groups mostly around garbage dumps.

Where found: Large tracts of wooded areas of North America, north of
central Mexico.

About the Author

Bobbie Hamsa was born and raised in Nebraska, far away from any far-fetched pets. Mrs. Hamsa has a Bachelor of Arts Degree in English Literature from the University of Nebraska. She is married and has a son, John.

Mrs. Hamsa is an advertising copywriter in Omaha. She writes print, radio, and television copy for a full range of accounts, including Mutual of Omaha's "Wild Kingdom," the five-time Emmy Award winning wild animal series and sometime resource for far-fetched pets.

About the Artist:

Tom Dunnington divides his time between book illustration and wildlife painting. He has done many books for Childrens Press, as well as working on textbooks, and is a regular contributor to "Highlights for Children." He is at present working on his "Endangered Wildlife" series, which is being reproduced as limited edition prints. Tom lives in Elmhurst, Illinois.